Plate 1 (on front cover). Detail from "SETTING LAMPS ADRIFT."
1909. (See Plate 10.)

KODANSHA LIBRARY OF JAPANESE ART

No. 4

Plate 2. YOKOYAMA TAIKAN. *Photograph.*

横 山 大 観

YOKOYAMA TAIKAN

(*1868 —*)

Text by
SEIROKU NOMA

English adaptation by
MEREDITH WEATHERBY

CHARLES E. TUTTLE COMPANY
Rutland, Vermont — Tokyo, Japan

NOTE ON THE ENGLISH TEXT

The name of Taikan is practically a household word in Japan, where it requires little introduction. In preparing this text for readers not so familiar with the man and his work, however, I have needed more basic information than that supplied in Mr. Noma's excellent but interpretive text in the Japanese edition. Therefore I gratefully acknowledge having drawn liberally on an article by the same author in the *Japan Quarterly* and having taken information from *Time's* recent report (see Bibliography). I have been greatly assisted by the collaboration of Miss Kyoko Kaneko. Throughout the book all Japanese names are given with surname first.

M. W.

Published by the Charles E. Tuttle Company, of Rutland, Vermont & Tokyo, Japan, by arrangement with Kodansha, Tokyo. All rights reserved by Kodansha, without whose written permission no part of the contents of this book may be reproduced.

First English edition, February, 1956

Third printing, 1959

Library of Congress Catalog Card No. 56-8489

Printed in Japan by
Toppan Printing Co., Ltd., Tokyo

YOKOYAMA TAIKAN

Ironically, Yokoyama Taikan, who was to become one of the great champions of Japanese tradition, was born in 1868, the very year which marked Japan's major revolt against tradition. Only a few years earlier Admiral Perry had forced the feudalistic Tokugawa regime to open the country after more than two centuries of hermit-like seclusion, and with the restoration of imperial power in 1868 Japan turned her back resolutely on the past, entering that amazing period of Westernization which was to make her a modern nation in only a few decades. This period also saw such an infatuation with anything and everything Western that Japanese culture came to be held in low repute.

Art was no exception. The greatest of Oriental master-pieces were being thrown on rubbish heaps or hawked about the streets for pittances. Fortunately, at this point there appeared a small group of far-seeing men to oppose the mob and gradually win for Japanese art, both in the West and—with more difficulty—in Japan, the esteem it deserved. Notable among these were Ernest Fenollosa, the great American authority on Japanese art and long-time teacher in Japan, and his disciple Okakura Tenshin, whose determined efforts led to the establishment of the Tokyo School of Fine Arts in 1889, headed by Okakura and dedicated to the growth of a truly Japanese art based firmly upon Japanese tradition.

Taikan was among the first students to enroll in the new school. His stormy life had characteristically begun in a bamboo grove, where his mother had crept to escape a political battle raging in their village. As a young boy he had moved with his parents to the metropolis of Tokyo and been sent to a school of English to prepare for government service. He had, however, loved painting since boyhood, and now he turned to art over the fierce opposition of his father, a former samurai of the Mito clan.

His years of study at the School of Fine Arts were decisive ones, determining the future course of his life. From Okakura, an art theorist rather than an artist, he acquired the philosophy and the ideals which he has followed unswervingly now for more than sixty years. From Hashimoto Gaho, a great traditional artist and eminent teacher, he acquired his firm mastery of the brush in all its traditional brilliance, as well as a bold willingness to experiment. And he also acquired a Homeric capacity for saké. Okakura's advice was that an artist should either not drink at all or else drink abundantly, a dictum Taikan took so much to heart that even now he still drinks two quarts of his favorite brand, "Inebriate Soul," a day, feeding his dog most of the food that his wife vainly urges upon him. He attributes both his painting name of Taikan, "Great Outlook," as well as much of his artistic inspiration to his love for saké, but makes it a strict rule never to drink while painting.

With all his proven talent and unusually competent teachers, Taikan seemed to have an unlimited future before him. For a long time, however, things did not go well. Okakura was forced out of the School of Fine Arts in 1898 by opponents of his principles, and some thirty other teachers and employees of the college, including Taikan, by then an assistant professor, resigned their positions to follow their master. Determined to carry on Okakura's work, this resolute group formed the Japanese Academy of Art in spite of the fact that they had neither governmental nor popular support.

During this period Taikan, inspired both by the precepts

Plate 3. CH'U YUAN. *Color on silk. A section.* 1898. *(See explanation following Plate 32.)*

of his teacher Hashimoto, who had been struggling with old techniques in order to revitalize native Japanese painting, and by his own desire to coax the public back to an appreciation of the old art, began attempting to separate the component elements of the ancient style and reassemble them in novel ways. For example, he boldly cast aside line, the most prominent feature of Oriental painting, and devised what came to be called the "dimness" style, of which the "Lost Child" is a good example. But his experiments pleased neither the conservatives, who called them desecrations of the Oriental spirit, nor the general public. In the meantime the members of the Academy had been falling away, until it was reduced to a mere handful living in a small coastal village, working constantly to perfect their painting styles, and earning a bare livelihood by trading paintings for rice.

The Academy did receive some slight recognition for its perseverance in the face of overwhelming difficulties when Taikan was appointed to the jury which selected works to be shown in the prestigious annual exhibits organized by the Ministry of Education. But by 1913, the year of Okakura's death, most of the other founders of the Academy were dead or had deserted, and the end of the experiment seemed at hand. All these hardships, however, only inspired Taikan to work the harder, and following in his master's footsteps, he reorganized the Academy practically single-handedly. His spirited and energetic leadership attracted a group of young, ambitious artists, and gradually the Academy became the talk of the artistic world, became in fact the new impetus to modern painting which Okakura had intended it to be. Thus Taikan's place in the vanguard of Japan's art world was at last firmly established, especially after the exhibition in 1923 of his masterly and tremendously popular scroll, "The Wheel of Life."

In the years since then Taikan has never lost sight of his first goal; through many changes of style and to the

Plate 4. Lost Child. *Charcoal on silk. Detail. 1902. (See explanation following Plate 32.)*

accompaniment of steadily growing acclaim he has always continued working for the development and glory of the Japanese style. A fiercely independent man of monumental rages, Taikan shows his forceful personality in his appearance and conduct. His hair is unkempt because he cuts it himself, having become impatient with barbers in his youth. He always wears traditional Japanese clothing, even when traveling abroad, and claims never to have sat in a chair. Saying, "In the West most artists paint with the eye; in the East, with the soul," he works from memory in his studio and even at the age of eighty-seven shows a vigor which a man half his age might well envy.

Taikan is a great believer in his own nation, a "nationalist" and a "traditionalist," but always in his own distinctive way, and always without narrow-mindedness or prejudice. He knows more about the ways of foreign countries than most other Japanese, having traveled abroad on many occasions, first to India in 1903 and as late as 1930 as an artistic ambassador to Italy. His travels have given him a broad view of the world and have also strengthened his belief that the Japanese can make no contribution to world culture unless they remain truly Japanese in spirit.

Taikan likes best to paint monochromes in Chinese ink, no doubt because they reveal the best qualities of Oriental art, but he excels in colors as well, having perfected his black-and-white style only after much experimentation in many styles and much work in color. His visits to India, Europe, America, and China all had their influences, and he gradually forsook his "dimness" style to return to a more traditional use of line, but only in his own time and not because of the hostility his experiments encountered. Turning to color, he began first with very light washes, gradually progressing to ever heavier, ever thicker colors. His "Mountain Path" represented a completely new conception of tone colors in Japanese art and formed the basis for a whole new

ate 5. LOA-TZU. *Color on silk. A section. 1921.*

system of coloring, which has had a lasting influence on subsequent color harmony. In "Plenty of Room for the Knife" Taikan made still more startling innovations in full, bold color, and finally, in such pictures as "Maple Leaves," he turned to a gorgeous and purely decorative use of color.

The expert sense of coloring which he displayed in these works of his colorful period—works, incidentally, which would have assured him a place among Japan's masters even if he had painted nothing more—may make it seem strange that he next turned to monochrome, but it was precisely this sense of color which enabled him to see the endless tonal possibilities of black. No pigments can ever reproduce the myriad color variations of nature, and the painter who works with colors must therefore employ a certain amount of deception to make up for the deficiencies of pigment. How much simpler and more natural then—if also more difficult—to change the infinite colors of the spectrum into subtle shades of black and white. Thus Taikan's preference for ink arises out of his desire to be more faithful to nature. And when he turned to monochrome he not only mastered the traditions of the past, but also opened new vistas for its future development.

As early as 1911 Taikan had produced two scroll paintings in monochrome based upon his travels in China. Revealing his complete mastery of traditional brushwork, these also employed a new use of perspective and shadow to become a happy synthesis of Occidental and Oriental techniques. This in itself was a tremendous achievement, but he was still determined to discover a completely new and original style. This he did in 1923 with the most ambitious "Wheel of Life," painted in monochrome at the very height of his experiments in vivid color. Here, however, ink was his only color, and he relied on simplification and symbolism for his effect, using the analogy of flowing water to portray the unceasing movement of the cosmos itself, with people

late 6. CH'U-SHUI SCROLL. *Ink on paper. A section. 1910.*

and animals interwoven in a magnificent pattern of universal rhythm. The tremendous success of the painting lies in his having made full use of a medium that is ideal for expressing spiritual values. It first went on display only a few hours before the great Tokyo earthquake, but fortunately escaped destruction and did much to make people see once again the beauties of monochrome painting, an art that had all but been forgotten by the public.

Since "The Wheel of Life" Taikan has continued his work in monochrome, developing many styles, sometimes elegant and calm, sometimes whispering, reaching a stage

Plate 7. YEN-SHAN AND CH'ANG-CHIANG SCROLL. *Ink in paper.*
Section from "Ch'ang-chiang." 1911.

of originality truly beyond compare. Early in his monochrome period he abandoned realism, also attempting to suppress all tricks of technical virtuosity. And soon he began to add body to his monochromes by applying coat after coat of ink. Scenes drawn in this new style, such as his 1928 "Waterfall," give the impression of immovable strength, being notable for the jet black of their ink as well as for their complicated tonal nuances.

Still not satisfied, however, Taikan moved on next to monochromes with a soft, liquid touch replacing the strong heavy blacks, showing that behind the stern spirit of the ancient warrior there lay the romantic nature of the poet. By using soft, lyrical shading he sought to develop those characteristics of Oriental painting which were native to Japan rather than importations from China. In complete contrast to his earlier works, his paintings now were gentle and full of sentiment, showing greater depth of poetic insight than his earlier monochromes, achieved by a technique of shading so masterful that other painters have not even been able to approximate it.

Thus it is that Taikan's monochrome paintings have come to be regarded as the pinnacle of his art. And yet it must never be forgotten that he came to black and white by the way of color. It is precisely because of his unusual color sense, on which his monochromes are firmly based, that his black has so many flavors and values.

In his choice of subjects Taikan has experimented almost as much as in his techniques. This may be attributed in part to his long life, but credit must also be given to his constant quest for new themes, new approaches to the mysteries of art. In his early years he painted many historical figures, influenced by Okakura's emphasis upon the Oriental past and by his own painstaking studies of the old masters. Later he turned to figures from everyday life, as for example in "Wildflowers." Although he has seldom given exclusive

Plate 8. YEN-SHAN AND CH'ANG-CHIANG SCROLL. *Ink on paper.*
Section from "Yen-shan." 1911.

attention to flowers and animals, subjects traditionally dear
to the Oriental artist, his larger pictures reveal many
surpassingly fine flower and animal details.

But when all is said and done it is still in the field of
landscape painting—and generally in monochrome—that
Taikan has done his most characteristic work. His talents
in this direction showed themselves early in his career, in the
two black-and-white scrolls based upon his trip to China, and
shortly thereafter in the colored scrolls showing scenes of

(continued following Plate 41)

Plate 9

SELFLESSNESS

Color on silk. Scroll for hanging. 1897.

This was exhibited when Taikan was thirty and, proving a large success, is famous as the work which first brought him fame. It shows a young boy at the waterside, wearing the wide-sleeved, oversize kimono of the Heian period (782–1185). The pattern and cut of the kimono reveal the thoroughness with which Taikan had studied the past, even to the details of classical costumes, while the skillful use of line and the serene yet gay coloring owe much to the old masters he was then studying by making careful copies of their works.

Selflessness is an ideal of Zen Buddhism, and it is interesting that Taikan should have chosen the figure of a young boy, standing selflessly, with the wide world stretching away around him, to represent this ideal. The same spirit is found in his choice of an artistic name—Taikan, "Great Outlook." The budding willows indicate that the season is spring. One interpretation of the picture, consonant with Taikan's character, might be that the heart that pursues the ideal of selflessness is a heart that will also dare to die proudly.

Plate 10

SETTING LAMPS ADRIFT

Color on silk. Section of a scroll for hanging. 1909. (See detail on cover.)

In 1903, on the advice of his teacher Okakura, Taikan went on a trip to India. This was his first view of the outside world, and he was deeply impressed with Indian customs and manners. This picture is based upon his Indian travels, showing three unmarried girls of Benares engaged in the custom of setting boat-shaped lamps adrift on the Ganges, watching hopefully to foretell their future happiness by whether the lamps floated out of sight or—a bad sign— overturned. Japan has a somewhat similar lamp-floating custom, but it generally has a more festive air, and Taikan was doubtlessly struck by the intent expressions on the faces of the Indian girls. The reproduction here shows the full width of the picture, but omits a charmingly composed detail of vines and leaves aboves the girls' heads, as well as the barest suggestion of flowing river at their feet.

Until going to India Taikan had been working in his so-called "dimness" style, but his travels seem to have both purified his painting mood and added something refreshing to his tone and technique, which represented an important step forward toward his maturity. Many of his works showing his impressions of India have been lost, and it is most fortunate that this excellent example of an important turning point in his style was recently rediscovered.

Plate 11

MASTER FIVE-WILLOWS

Color over gold on silk. Section of a screen. 1912.

Master Wu-liu (Five-Willows) was the famous Chinese poet of the Chin dynasty, T'ao Yuan-ming. Refusing to sacrifice his principles to keep his position as a government official, he wrote a famous poem on the subject of returning to the country after resigning from the government and, abandoning fame and wealth, did indeed retire to his native province to enjoy a quiet life of tippling and poetry making.

The section seen here shows the left end of the screen, where the poet walks proudly. The right end shows a serving boy carrying the Chinese harp which T'ao Yuan-ming was fond of playing. A wide blank space separates the two figures, suggesting both the lonely nature of the poet and the wideness of the world inhabited by a man who refuses to sacrifice principles. There is an air of nobility about this representation of the poet with his skirts blowing in the wind.

In choosing this subject Taikan was certainly thinking of his teacher Okakura, driven out of the presidency of the governmental Tokyo School of Fine Arts for his inflexible principles, but Taikan probably also had in mind his own desire to pursue his ideals without having to curry official favor. The figure of Ch'u Yuan in a similar pose (Plate 3), striding before the wind, is one of bitterness, whereas this somehow gives the feeling of hopefulness.

Plate 12

SEN NO YOSHIRO

Color on silk. Section of a screen. 1918.

Probably the most revered of all Japan's masters of the tea
ceremony and flower arrangement is Sen Rikyu (1520–1591).
This picture shows an episode in the early life of the master,
while he was still a student with the name Yoshiro.   One
day, after carefully sweeping the garden for expected visi-
tors, he purposely left two or three leaves lying on the
ground.   His master praised him greatly, saying his action
revealed a deep understanding of the spirit of the tea cult.

It is interesting, perhaps even paradoxical, that Taikan, a
devotee of a more robust drink, should have chosen a tea-
ceremony subject.   But then perhaps it is not surprising
after all, for both Taikan and Rikyu reveal the same love
of childlike awkwardness and deliberate informality.   Taikan
showed great originality in picturing the great tea master
as a robust young man instead of the old, emaciated hermit
which most pictures of him show.

Plate 13

WILDFLOWERS

Color on paper.   Section of a screen.   1936.

The section is reproduced from the right side of a pair of screens, each comprised of two panels, while the detail shown in Plate 21 is from the left side of the pair. In subject matter these screens, showing the beauties of everyday life, lie midway between Taikan's historical subjects and his later, philosophical landscapes.   The left-hand screen shows an artfully informal composition of autumn flowers and grasses, while in the right-hand screen attention centers upon this human flower in the form of a country working woman.   Taikan seems here to be chiding the world for the way it so often disregards the simpler beauties to be found in rural nature.   Painting from memory as he usually does, Taikan must have a prodigious memory to produce a feeling of such on-the-spot immediacy.   Without doubt he was here remembering having seen just such a woman as this, with her refreshing navy-blue clothing and her clear eyes.   Technically, the picture is interesting both for the coloring of the kimono and the skillful use of line to suggest the texture and weight of the bank in the background.

The left-hand screen (Plate 21) is a representative example of Taikan's treatment of flowers, showing how, unlike other painters of flowers, he first observes nature carefully and then, not sketching directly from nature, ideates what he has seen, allowing his observations to be distilled in his own mind before putting them on paper.

Plates 14–16

PLENTY OF ROOM FOR THE KNIFE

Color on silk. Set of two scrolls for hanging. 1914.

This is another historical subject, based upon a story in Chuang-tzu's treatise on taking care of one's health. One day Wen Hui-chun asked his extremely skillful cook the secret of cooking. The cook replied that there are always interstices in any piece of meat and that, on the other hand, a knife has no thickness. Hence there is always "plenty of room for the knife"—a famous Oriental saying meaning roughly "it's easy if you know how" or, in a deeper sense, that any great skill must be exercised without strain, with disinterest even.

The fact that Taikan painted this picture for the first exhibition held by the Japanese Academy of Art after its reorganization under his leadership indicates the deep impression this saying made upon him. Certainly Oriental paintings are executed with more spirit of "plenty of room for the knife" than are the more studied and painstaking Western-style paintings.

Taikan has given the blue-robed cook a face sufficiently strong to convince the beholder that he might indeed have spoken those very words. The coloring also is worthy of note, the thickness and boldness being at that time a novel innovation in Japanese painting. The clear and beautiful tones of the clothing of Wen Hui-chun and his consort provide a lovely contrast with the strongly molded blue of the clothing covering the cook's lean body and the brown massiveness of the carving block.

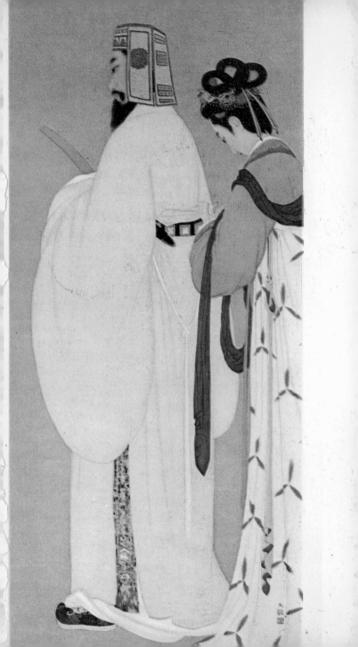

Plate 17

IN THE SHADE OF THE WILLOWS

Color gold on silk. Section of a screen. 1913.

The entire screen is covered with luxurious willows, painted against a golden background, and seems to produce a choked scent of green foliage on a hot summer day. There is a brook running through the trees on the left side of the screen, giving a sense of cool relief. Inside the house beside the brook can be seen the host and a guest, chatting pleasantly, unconscious of the heat. The guest might well be the Master Wu-liu of Plate 11, who was particularly fond of willows and also of visiting about the countryside to drink wine with his rural neighbors.

The section reproduced here is from the right-hand side of the screen, showing a servant boy who has pulled his donkey into the shade of the willow tree and is taking a nap, a fact which makes us still more aware of the lengthy chat which has been going on inside the house between the boy's master and the host, and of the heat which pervades the entire scene. This particular detail, suggesting as it does that there is more of purity and guilelessness in the face of the sleeping boy than in the idle chatter of the men in the house, is representative of Taikan's admiration for the mind of childhood, as already seen in "Selflessness" (Plate 9). Taikan's admiration for the selflessness and naiveté of childhood has been expressed in a number of paintings of sleeping children.

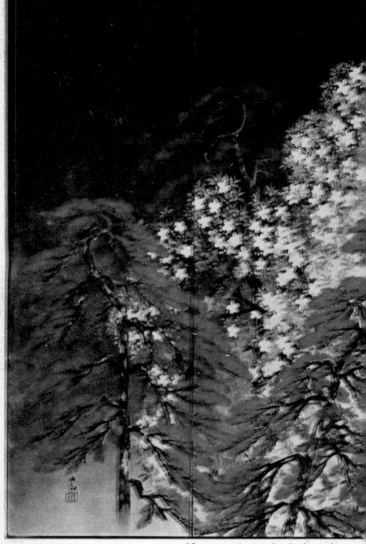

Plate 18. CHERRY BLOSSOMS AT NIGHT. *The left-hand of a pair of screens. 1929. (See following plate.)*

Plate 19. CHERRY BLOSSOMS AT NIGHT. *Forms a pair with the preceding, being the right-hand side. (See explanation following Plate 32.)*

Plate 20

AUTUMN COLORS

Color on silk backed with gold.   Section of a screen.   1917.

Taikan made a deep study of the gay decorativeness and symbolic simplicity of the Korin school and then went on to use these techniques in new and bright color combinations, as may be seen here. The two deer are beautifully placed beneath an arrangement of arrowroot leaves suggestive of autumn in the mountains. Tipping the green leaves with yellow and red was a particularly successful way of avoiding the static quality often found in pictures of autumn foliage and indicating the constant changing of colors. The jewel-like berries of the plant combine with the leaves to make a Gobelin tapestry of the picture.

Shimomura Kanzan also painted pictures in the manner of the Korin school, but Taikan alone was able to use the Korin technique and still suggest a fullness, a dimension of depth completely new to the style. He knew, in short, how to repeat a single subdued note until it became a full symphony. Note particularly how the deer are simplified, and yet have texture and fullness—a feat revealing the full measure of the artist and his keen observation of nature. It is this very process of simplifying after having once penetrated to the core of his subject that led naturally to the black-and-white paintings which would shortly follow, just as the increasingly gorgeous use of colors were likewise leading him on to even more startling shades in black and white.

Plate 21. WILDFLOWERS. Color on paper. Section of a screen. 1936. (See Plate 13 for explanation.)

Plate 22

RED PERSIMMON LEAVES

Color on silk backed with gold.   Section of a screen.   1920.

Here again Taikan made use of the techniques of the Korin
school. But unlike "Autumn Colors" (Plate 20), painted
some three years earlier in thick colors, this shows a different concept of autumn foliage, the leaves being painted
in thin colors. Taikan had now reached the climax in his
use of colors and was gradually moving toward black and
white. More than the pictures with bolder colors, such a
picture as this reveals the extreme delicacy of his color
sense. The use of black ink in the painting of the branches
here is interesting, providing an effective contrast with the
 hin colors of the leaves.

Plate 23

RED MAPLE LEAVES

Color on paper. Section of a screen. 1931.

This is Taikan's last work in the style of the Korin school. The entire screen shows two large old maple trees, in full autumn glory, stretching their interestingly shaped branches over a clear brook. The water itself is done in ultramarine, with a wave pattern of powdered platinum, producing a pure and cold background for the flaming red of the maple leaves. Blank spaces in the composition are flaked with platinum to produce a total effect that is altogether brilliant and gorgeous.

It is surprising to realize that this was painted at the age of sixty-four, when Taikan was already deep in his monochrome period. It was at this time that the artist was caught in the conflict between his love of colors and the increasing attraction he was feeling for black and white, and yet somehow, as this example shows, his interest in the new style had not lessened any of the loving care and talent he put into the old.

Plate 24. QUAIL. *Detail from "Red Persimmon Leaves" (Plate 22).*
The screen on which this detail appears shows, in addition
to the red persimmon leaves of Plate 22, a bamboo grove,
in the midst of which this solitary quail appears. The
bird is depicted with unusual precision for Taikan, who
generally tended toward simplification; this is much more
in the style of classical masters of the bird-and-flower style.
The bird was the last touch added to the screen, its position
having merely been indicated by a vague charcoal circle
until two or three days before the work's completion, a
fact which indicates how much thought the artist must
have given to the detail before finally executing it, quickly
and surely. This was indeed a happy touch for the composition as a whole, providing a welcome relief from the
bleakness of the cold autumn scene.

Plate 25. WAGTAIL. *Detail from "Red Maple Leaves" (Plate 23).*
Perhaps the frequent birds and animals which Taikan shows
in his landscapes are symbols of the playful side of his own
nature. However that may be, they always have the fortunate result of giving additional life and movement to what
might otherwise be too weighty a scene. As in the case
of the quail of the preceding plate, this bird too is precisely rendered, being another example of the wide variety
of techniques Taikan had available at the tip of his brush.
This wagtail appears on the right side of the screen, flying
away toward the sky above the brook against a platinum-
flecked background. Many representations of flying birds
look like so many pieces of paper cut out and pasted on;
only the touch of a master could give such a real sense of
of flight as is found here.

← LIFT FOLD

Plate 26

MOUNTAIN PATH

Color on paper. Detail from a scroll for hanging. 1911.

A mountain path on an autumn evening. A horse is being led home by its driver. The surrounding trees reflect an infinite variety of color. One can imagine that the leaves are rustling crisply in the mountain breeze, and that the horseman has been singing a lusty song, punctuated by the clip-clop of the horse's hooves. The day's work is ended, and the man's cheerful voice resounded in the calm, lonely countryside. The whole scene is brought to life so vividly that the viewer imagines he can hear the sounds, smell the the autumn air, even share the feelings of the man and his horse.

This picture was exhibited in 1911 at the annual exhibit sponsored by the Ministry of Education and did much to establish Taikan's fame in the world of Japanese art. Its tonal colors are reminiscent of *yamato-e*, but its bold and rhythmical use of mineral pigments represented a completely new departure in Japanese art and was to have tremendous influence.

Plates 27 & 28

UJI RIVER PICTURE SCROLL

Color on silk.   Sections of a horizontal scroll.   1919.

The horizontal picture scroll developed in ancient times
from scroll manuscripts.   Although somewhat awkward to
display and likely to be damaged by careless viewers, it
has never disappeared entirely from Oriental art as it did
in the West, probably because the possibilities it offers for
dynamic continuity and flow are peculiarly well suited to
the Oriental style.   Doubtless the classical associations of
the form appealed to Taikan, who favors it greatly, having
produced some of his best works on horizontal scrolls.

This particular scroll is a lyrically rendered painting of
scenes along the banks of the historic Uji River which
finds its source in Lake Biwa near Kyoto.   The soft ele-
gance of the tones were intricately produced by mineral
pigment over mineral pigment, all surmounted with a
structure of soft line drawing, which, surprisingly enough,
contributes to the lyrical effect.   Taikan is usually thought
of as having a sturdy, philosophical style, whereas this
picture reveals another side of his many-faceted personality
—delicacy and sentiment.   Thus this picture forms an interesting contrast, both in subject matter and treatment, with
the magnificent "Wheel of Life" (Plates 33 & 34).

Plate 28. UJI RIVER PICTURE SCROLL. *A section. See preceding plate.*

Plate 29

ARA RIVER SCROLL

Color on paper. Section of a horizontal scroll. 1915.

The scene reproduced shows a ferry on the upper reaches
of the Ara, a river in the Tokyo area. One can imagine
how rapidly the woman and her child must have run down
to the bank of the river, only to find the ferryman had
just shoved off without them. This is a good example of
how Taikan could give most of his attention to the landscape, and still have a friendly eye for the human beings
in it, a talent he was to develop still further in "The
Wheel of Life."

The technique used here is one of thin black lines and
thin colors of mineral pigments. The ease and informality
of the style, with its flowing brush strokes, shows a happy
fusion of the native Japanese *yamato-e* style and that of
the Southern school of Chinese painting.

Plate 30

LANDSCAPES IN THE FOUR SEASONS

Color on paper. Section of a horizontal scroll. 1947.

The feeling and mood of Japan's famous scenery vary markedly with the seasons, a fact which Taikan captures in this scroll showing the natural beauties of his motherland. The portion reproduced here shows a deep gorge and clear river in midsummer. Painted in his eightieth year, during the difficult and confused period which followed Japan's defeat in war and the Allied occupation of the country, this provides an interesting contrast with "The Resplendent Isles" scroll, painted on a similar subject only a few years earlier, but before Japan had embarked upon its disastrous war. Unlike the earlier work, this contains no eulogy on Japanese history. In an ancient Chinese poem it is said that even though the nation be defeated, the mountains and rivers remain ; this new scroll was doubtlessly inspired by this sentiment, and the artist revealed in it the saddened spirit of a great patriot. Rather than depict his subject entirely in ink, however, this time he included a certain amount of color, perhaps to ward off sorrowful feelings.

Thus, though the ultimate object of the picture is practically the same as that of "The Resplendent Isles," the approach is quite different. Though still using the soft black of the Southern Chinese school, at the same time he added thick and beautiful spots of color, revealing yet another important style.

Plates 31 & 32

THE MOUNTAIN IN FRESH COLORS

Color on silk.   A scroll for hanging.   1928.

Taikan has always tended toward symbolism, and it is for
this reason as much as for Mt. Fuji's eminently paintable
shape that he has drawn more pictures of it than any
Japanese artist, more even than did Hokusai.   But then
Hokusai, while deeply interested in Fuji's changing appear-
ances, regarded it essentially as only scenery.   Taikan, on
the other hand, looks upon it as a symbol of his nation,
and his whole concept of Japan is symbolized in his representations of the mountain.

Taikan first began painting Fuji around 1915, and by
the time this particular work was done his "Fuji" style
had considerably mellowed.   Here he combines black, in
both maximum thickness and hazy thinness, with Taikan's
favored powdered pigments forming the smoky clouds.   The
beautifully executed pine trees in the foreground allow the
mountain to be seen in the full freshness and sublimity of
its coloring.

Plate 3. CH'U YUAN Painted in 1898, this is one of Taikan's early historical subjects. Ch'u Yuan was a loyal minister of a Chinese prince in the third century B.C.; the story goes that, slandered by envious rivals and misunderstood by his prince, he gave vent to his just resentment in a series of poems and then drowned himself in despair. Taikan painted this picture the year his teacher and spiritual guide, Oka-kura Tenshin, was forced out of the presidency of the Tokyo School of Fine Arts; it was shown at the first ex-hibit of the new Academy of Art, formed by Okakura's followers to carry on his work. Both in choice of subject and in execution Taikan was revealing the bitterness of his feelings over the way Okakura had been treated. The portion of the painting reproduced here shows the full height of the picture, but omits a delicate suggestion of the desolation of nature found on the right half of the picture, the solitary human form of Ch'u Yuan being placed well toward the left edge. This picture offers interesting contrasts with "Master Five-Willows" (Plate 11).

Plate 4. LOST CHILD. The entire picture shows a bewildered child surrounded by four figures—Confucius, Buddha, Christ, and Lao-tzu—and was Taikan's satirical comment upon the intellectual confusion then prevalent in Japan. The detail shown is a representative example of Taikan's "dimness" style, in which he discarded the characteristic Oriental use of line.

Plate 18 & 19. CHERRY BLOSSOMS AT NIGHT. This magnificent pair of six-panel screens was painted for the Japanese Fine Arts Exhibit held at Rome in 1930, which Taikan attended in person, and occupies an important position among Taikan's works. The virile and massive composition overflows with a spirit of nobility and was indeed a fine choice to send abroad as a representative work of modern Japanese art. Here in a single work both Taikan's unusual sense of colors and his characteristic technique in black Chinese ink are skillfully combined to produce a fantastically beautiful scene of a spring evening in Kyoto. No human beings are present, but the fires lit to illuminate the cherry blossoms at night suggest the presence of people, while the grandeur of the composition suggests the mutability of human pleasure when compared with the eternal qualities of nature and the universe.

Plates 33 & 34. THE WHEEL OF LIFE. This black-and-white scroll, over one hundred and thirty feet long, is undoubtedly one of Taikan's greatest masterpieces. The scroll begins with a scene in the mountains remote from all signs of human life; a tiny rivulet condenses from the mist and, joining with other streams, becomes a great river. Emerging from the mountains, it flows through populated regions to the ocean, from which it rises again as mist and returns inland. This eternal process is the center of attention in the scroll, but the activities of people and animals are interwoven, so that one gets the impression of a magnificent universal rhythm.

Plate 33. THE WHEEL OF LIFE. *Ink on silk. Section of a scroll. 1923. (See preceding page for explanation.)*

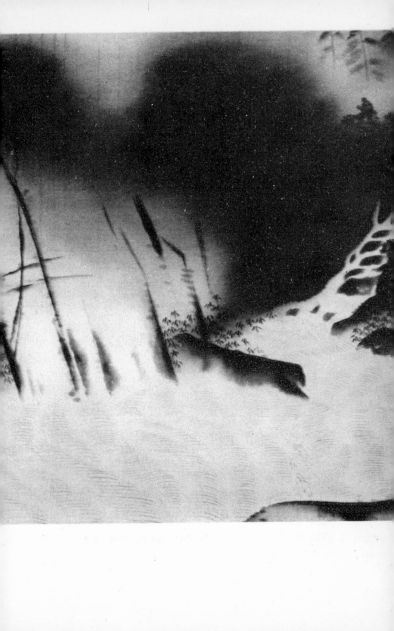

Plate 34. THE WHEEL OF LIFE. *Section. (See preceding plate.)*

海色秋月
大観

Plate 35. AUTUMN ON LAKE TUNG-T'ING. From "*Eight Views*"

Plate 36. CHICHIBU MOUNTAINS ON A SPRING MORNING. *Ink and gold on silk. 1928.*

Plate 37. WATERFALL. Ink on silk. Forms a pair with the following. 1928.

Plate 38. WATERFALL. *Ink on silk. Forms a pair with the preceding.* 1928.

Plate 39. EARLY SUMMER. *Color on paper. 1940.*

Plate 40. MOONLESS MID-AUTUMN NIGHT. *Color on paper. Scroll for hanging.* 943. Based on a poem of the same title by Okakura Tenshin, which may be but poorly paraphrased: "In a world of dreams, in a dream f the world, crying and laughing, laughing and crying, and the tears vhich remain are drops of dew. Of what does the cricket sing — 'Chin, hin, chin, chi-ro-rin, drown, drown, drown, earth-dew-lonesomeness'? Iow desolate the autumn without a moon."

Plate 41. THE RESPLENDENT ISLES. *Thin colors on paper. Section of a horizontal scroll. 1941.*

(continued from page preceding Plate 9)

his own country such as "Uji River" and "Ara River." With the nobly conceived "Wheel of Life" and "Eight Views of Hsiao-Hsiang" his landscape art made a bold leap to reach its flowering. Then, at the age of seventy-three, he startled everyone with the amazing display of vitality seen in "The Resplendent Isles," a monumental scroll done in honor of the 2,600th anniversary of the founding of Japan. This presents a vast aerial panorama of Japanese scenes, composed with the nation's history in mind, and was clearly painted with all the artist's fervor and strength.

A short while later the country he had so lovingly painted was reduced by misguided politics to a state of ruin and confusion. He himself lost his house during an air raid. Even so his artistic passion was not dampened. In 1947 he produced the long scroll "Landscapes in the Four Seasons," and in 1949 the painting "Jewel Wrapped in Rags," which showed a Chinese priest dressed in tattered clothing and was Taikan's eloquent plea to his countrymen to maintain their strength of character even in the face of destitution.

Taikan has always tended toward symbolism, and it is for this reason that he has drawn so many pictures of Mt. Fuji—more than any other Japanese artist. He regards the mountain as a symbol of his nation, and his whole concept of Japan is symbolized in his presentations of the mountain.

There is probably no other person who has played such an important part in the development of modern Japanese art as Taikan. No other painter has used such a variety of styles, or produced so many significant works, or approached him in spiritual character. And he is by no means a man of the past. On the contrary, even at the age of eighty-seven, still strong and vital, he is still attempting to reach new horizons. Upon reaching his eighty-eighth year he said that the congratulations he was receiving from all over the world were but alarm bells reminding him that he had as yet barely scratched the surface of art.

BIOGRAPHICAL CHRONOLOGY

1868   Born September 17, in Mito, the eldest son of Sakai Sutehiko.

1889   Entered the newly established Tokyo School of Fine Arts, of which Okakura Tenshin was head.

1893   Graduated.

1895   Appointed an Assistant Professor at the School. Visited many shrines and temples, copying the old masters.

1898   Resigned from the School upon Okakura's dismissal. Joined the newly formed Japanese Academy of Art.

1903   Traveled in India. Visited the poet Tagore.

1904   The Academy was facing difficulties. Traveled in America.

1906   The Academy was foundering. Moved to Izura, in Ibaragi Prefecture, with the few remaining members. Worked hard on style.

1907   Appointed to the selections committee of the annual Ministry of Education art exhibit. The Academy was still facing great hostility.

1910   Traveled in China.

1913   Okakura died. Taikan reorganized the Academy.

1923   Tremendous success with "The Wheel of Life."

1930   Went to Rome as a cultural ambassador.

1931   Appointed artist to the Imperial Household.

1937   First recipient of Japan's Culture Medal.

1940   Presented "Ten Views of Seas and Mountains" to the Emperor.

1941   Presented "The Resplendent Isles" to the Emperor in commemoration of the 2,600th anniversary of the founding of Japan.

1947   Displayed "Landscapes in the Four Seasons" at the 32nd exhibition of the Japanese Academy of Art.

1955   Widely congratulated on his 87th birthday.

BIBLIOGRAPHY

Taikan Sakuhin Shu (Collection of Taikan's Works). Otsuka Kogeisha, Tokyo, 1925.

Zoku Taikan Sakuhin Shu (Collection of Taikan's Works Continued). Otsuka Kogeisha, Tokyo, 1928.

Nippon Bijutsuin Shi (History of the Japan Academy of Art), by Saito Ryuzo. Sogensha Tokyo, 1944.

Taikan Gadan (Taikan's World), an autobiography. Kodansha, Tokyo, 1951.

Taikan Gagyo Rokujunen Zuroku (Pictorial Record of Sixty Years of Taikan's Painting). Otsuka Kogeisha, Tokyo, 1950.

Taikan Fugaku Shu (Collection of Taikan's Mt. Fuji). Otsuka Kogeisha, Tokyo, 1954.

Taikan Byobu to Emaki Shu (Collection of Taikan's Screens and Picture Scrolls). Otsuka Kogeisha, Tokyo, 1955.

"Yokoyama Taikan," article in English by Noma Seiroku, *Japan Quarterly,* October-December. 1955, pp. 439–46.

"Great-Outlook Master," article in Pacific edition of *Time,* September 19, 1955, p. 42.